AGRIC BUSINESS CAN FAIL!

TUNDE BANJOKO

ADVANCE PRAISE FOR AGRIC BUSINESS CAN FAIL!

Although Agriculture started in the Garden of Eden, more as a survival means than a business, but it has never grown out of fashion.

However, those who approach farming only for money, just as in most business do not last. Mr Omotunde Banjoko has demonstrated his passion for Agriculture. I caught the bug like every other person who stayed long enough around him.

If you want to have a better understanding of Farming in all its forms, then you need to read this book in details.
Adebiyi Yinka
MD/CEO Nukadol Systems Ltd

When a single grain of maize is planted, it produces a minimum of one or two cobs for harvest. Each cob contains between two and five hundred grains. Meaning that with only one grain planted, one can reap five hundred grains on harvest. Such is the yield in farming as a business. Yet, quite a lot of farmers fail in the business.

The failure has been attributed to a lot of factors, some of which are the lack of deep knowledge of the art and the business of farming/agriculture.

This book has identified quite a number of the reasons for the failure of farmers in reaching their set targets or their desired heights in the business with proper solutions proffered to address the problems effectively.

Without doubt, the rich content of this book stands to improve the knowledge and skills of our teeming farming population and increase their productivity as to better meet the needs of our national population and even for export.

It is without hesitation that I began by personally applying the wealth of knowledge gained from reading it to improve my personal farming skills and also to recommend it to all farmers who are desirous of raising the bar of productivity in their work. Reading and applying the hints provided therein potentially draws much closer to reality, the achievements of the desire to reach the top.

I salute the author's efforts in putting the book together and convey the appreciation of my co-farmers as well as that of the entire nation, to him for the potential increase which the fantastic job stands to add to the gross domestic product of Nigeria.

Barr. Oloyede Oyediran
Principal Partner paradigm solicitors & Advocates

There are books and there are books. Coming across a very impactful, enriching, beneficial, life transforming, engaging and world-class book such as this is phenomenal.

Mr Omotunde Banjoko has brilliantly packaged this book highlighting the A- Z practical principles of how an AGRIC BUSINESS should be run successfully.
It covers succinctly areas on what Agric business is all about, myths about the business, business structure and stages, value chain, sources of capital, profitability and marketing.

I have a strong believe that success becomes very easy when you know what to do. The author has clearly stated all you need to know to be successful in this industry; simply put, mastering the AGRIC BUSINESS.

It is a must read! All operators in the Agric sector should get this book, and not just for themselves, but to buy as many copies as possible and bless others with it.
What are you still waiting for, go grab your copies and thank me immediately!
Abosede Fadayomi
Development Strategist
Terrain of Purpose

The difference between success and failure is knowledge, most times.

Right knowledge from the right source is the answer.

Omotunde Banjoko draws from wealth of experiential knowledge in Agric Business, information which guarantees success if properly and consistently applied.
Adegoke Akinola Adegbami
MD/CEO, Mainstreet Microfinance Bank, Author, Entrepreneur, Business and Leadership Coach

© 2017 Tunde Banjoko
+2348073312579
www.bofarmsltd.com
tundebanjoko@bofarmsltd.com
tundayb@gmail.com

At the time of going to press, every possible effort has been made to ensure that the information in this book is accurate, and does not constitute professional advice. Accordingly, the author, the publisher and agents shall not accept any responsibility for loss or damage occasioned to anyone acting, or refraining from acting as a result of the information in this publication.

Apart from any fair dealing for the purpose of research or review as permitted under the Copyright Laws, no part of this publication may be reproduced, stored in any system, or transmitted in any form or by any means, electronic, mechanical, photocopying, recording or otherwise without the prior permission of the author.

ISBN: 978-197-755-944-9

Tunde Banjoko

TABLE OF CONTENTS

FOREWORD *8*

INTRODUCTION *9*

CHAPTER 1: AGRICULTURE: THE FUTURE?............................... 12

CHAPTER 2: WHAT IS AGRICULTURAL BUSINESS?..................... 22

CHAPTER 3: WHY GO INTO AGRICULTURAL BUSINESS?............ 33

CHAPTER 4: GUIDE TO AGRICULTURAL BUSINESS..................... 38

CHAPTER 5: BEFORE YOU QUIT YOUR JOB FOR AGRICULTURAL BUSINESS.... 47

CHAPTER 6: STRUCTURE & STAGES OF AGRICULTURAL BUSINESS.......... 56

CHAPTER 7: SOURCES OF CAPITAL.. 72

CHAPTER 8: COMMUNITY RELATIONS & PROFITABILITY............ 80

ABOUT THE AUTHOR... 95

FOREWORD

Indeed agricultural business can fail like any other business venture.

However the author of this great book has demonstrated a great deal of passion to ensure that the guild lines highlighted could ensure the reader a soft landing and better planning and preparation.

I have extreme regards for the author whose passion for making positive impact in the agricultural sector is unstoppable.

Finally, I wish all readers of this great book, happy reading as you all apply the information practically as success comes your way.

Moses Babatunde Ogunyemi
MD/ CEO Thelma Farms

INTRODUCTION

Neglected and abandoned for so long, the business of agriculture is now a cash cow in Nigeria. Almost everyone is flocking towards it for the fortune that sector seems to promise. No doubt, it has become the toast of government at the state and federal levels, as well as a large percentage of the citizenry.

The sudden appeal of agric business is due in part to the plunging price of crude oil – the mainstay of the Nigerian economy – in the international market. As a result, throngs of people are trooping into agricultural business.

Unfortunately, a lot of the people showing interest in investing in this sector of the economy are either ill-equipped or lack requisite knowledge of the industry.

These people come into the industry with wrong assumptions and unrealistic expectations. They consider agriculture a get-rich-quick scheme. Mindsets such as these have made many new entrants into this industry fail to consider the various factors that will impact yield.

Unforeseen, and sometimes uncontrollable, situations like atmospheric conditions, erosion, and other peculiar cultural factors that farmers have to contend with, are not considered when huge returns are the main focus.

Surely, mouthwatering returns exist in the industry; but patience and adequate knowledge is what will bring the expected bumper returns.

It has become necessary, therefore, for new entrants into this business to sit and count the cost.

As a prospective participant in the agriculture value-chain, you need to ask yourself the following questions, and provide answers to them, before committing your time and resources:

- Is this intended as a side business? Or, is it a full-time business to which I can devote time and energy?
- Am I in this just to make money or to build a legacy?
- Am I presently looking for a business to engage in post-retirement that can sustain my present lifestyle even with improvements and flexibilities?

On gaining satisfactory answers to these questions, the next step is to decide the portion in the agriculture value chain where one's skillset and knowledge will be a perfect fit.

Unfortunately, from my interactions with a lot of people, I have observed that all these dynamics are not considered before they venture into the agriculture industry.

Then, after only a few months at best, millions of Naira has been flushed down the drain, as these people declare that the industry is not profitable.

It is my humble belief that this 'mishap' has come to a stop with the information you will gather from this book.

In this book, I share my experience in the industry to guide you, help you maximize profit and to safeguard your investments.

I also give you an overview of the different investment opportunities that are available in the industry.

After reading this book, you will come to see that farming is not only synonymous with owning or cultivating a land. Rather, you can center your business around transporting of agricultural produce, processing, exporting, storage, marketing, et al. These are all parts of the industry that are waiting to be fully explored.

The business of agriculture is profitable and exciting, only if you have the requisite and adequate knowledge which I will provide in this book

Chapter

CHAPTER 1
AGRICULTURE: THE FUTURE?

Picture this: An old man in tattered clothing wearing worn-out slippers, laboring day and night in the sun and in the cold on the farm. This man lives in a hut and sleeps on a mat with his wife and children.

The situation described above is the picture registered on the minds of many young people across Nigeria when the word *agriculture* is mentioned. These young people consider agriculture to be for the old and illiterate.

They rarely regard agriculture as a business or a thriving industry where wealth can be built like other 'more prestigious' professions like engineering, law, architecture, teaching, banking, trading, medicine, etc.

As a result, many people are not proud to introduce themselves as farmers in public gatherings. If they did introduce themselves as such, the picture that would pop up in the minds of their listeners is of someone who is living in a remote village and certainly wretched.

The good news is that this perception is fast changing. A lot more people are trooping into the industry and making good returns - just like the good old days of agriculture - than many people care to acknowledge in this modern day.

In those days before the oil boom, cash crops like palm produce (oil and kernel), cocoa, rubber, timber, groundnut, etc., powered the Nigerian economy. Jobs were created. Export flourished. Nigeria was not an import-dependent economy like we have it now.

It was during that period that the cocoa house in Ibadan was built. There was also the groundnut pyramid in the northern part of Nigeria, among other infrastructure that we enjoy till today. Some first generation universities too, were built by the proceeds from agricultural engagements.

If we could do all these before the oil boom, what went wrong? If agriculture was then able to bring out the glory of our nation, I believe the same can happen today. Agriculture has great potential to turn around the fortunes of Nigeria's fractured economy.

Analyst and experts have argued that if we attain our full potentials in agriculture, what the country is making in the oil and gas sector is nothing compared to what can be realized in the agricultural industry, if properly harnessed.

The individual states of the federation can generate more money than they presently receive as monthly allocations from Abuja.

In fact, some state governments in Nigeria can generate in four months what they do in a year, if agriculture is given the right place.

For example, in the western and eastern states of Nigeria where cash crops like cocoa is cultivated, as much as N10billion can be generated in a month from the sale of raw cocoa.

Rather pathetically, instead of latching on to these opportunities, these states are going cap-in-hand every month to collect billions of Naira in allocation from the federation account and yet are still owing workers their salaries.

> *AGRICULTURE HAS GREAT POTENTIAL TO TURN AROUND THE FORTUNES OF NIGERIA'S FRACTURED ECONOMY.*

In view of the potentials inherent in agriculture, it is my humble opinion that some of these states have no business going to Abuja in search of 'their share' of the federal allocation.

Agriculture compared to Oil & Gas

As a geophysicist, and active player in the downstream sector of the oil and gas industry, through painstaking research and my analyses, I can confidently submit that when properly harnessed, revenue from agriculture is very comparable and in some instance outweighs the one from oil and gas.

Furthermore, the security of investment in agriculture is greater than that in oil and gas, because each investor or participant has greater comparative control over the business.

Agric Business Can Fail!

The reason a lot of people don't realize agriculture is a goldmine is that they have failed to do a thorough analysis. If you sit down to do the analysis, you will discover that the returns on agriculture is huge. And this has been proven over time.

For example, you can earn as much as 100% returns on the raw sales of crops such as maize, cassava and some cash crops. When these crops have been processed, returns can climb to as high as 300%.

> THE REASON A LOT OF PEOPLE DON'T REALIZE AGRICULTURE IS A GOLDMINE IS THAT THEY HAVE FAILED TO DO A THOROUGH ANALYSIS.

When you compare how much one invests against the returns, the results are amazing. Ironically, this experience is what makes new entrants into this business to have challenges at the startup phase; because they focus on the figures and huge returns, then run with that information without asking the right questions.

For example, to cultivate cassava on 8 hectares of land, one may spend as much as N932, 000 (less land acquisition costs) and earn about N2, 400, 000 from raw sales only 12 months after.

However, engaging the same 8 hectares of land to cultivate cassava and this time, processing it could guarantee an output of about 240 tons of cassava. With this, one can earn as much as N7million, even assuming the lowest cost of *gari* per bag in Nigeria.

This estimate, of course, does not include the cost of land acquisition - I assume the land has been acquired or leased prior to cultivation. As you know, land is a fixed factor which will be prorated. So, if one can earn N7million as returns on a N932, 000 investment within a year, I think the return justifies the efforts – and to think that this is only on a calculation for 8 hectares of land.

It will interest you to know that there are companies in Nigeria cultivating over 400 hectares. Paltry International Ltd, for example, cultivates on a land area of over 400 hectares. Their profit is in the billion naira range. This is as listed on their website. Now, how many oil companies can declare that much returns today?

There are lots of big conglomerates in this country who are into rice production and generating more than this figure in a year.

There is another cocoa processing company in Ibadan, FTN Cocoa Processors Plc. Their assets are in the N20billion range. They don't even own a farm. All they do is blend and process the cocoa into semi-finished products and export.

Read this excerpt from their website:

> FTN Cocoa Processors Plc was formerly registered as Fantastic Traders Nigeria Limited, a Limited Liability Company which was incorporated in 1991. The company commenced cocoa processing business with a third-party arrangement (Toll Processing) with Stanmark Cocoa Processing Company Limited in 1995 for the conversion of cocoa beans into cocoa butter and cocoa cake/powder.
>
> The company later extended its third-party processing activities to Ile-Oluji Cocoa Cooperative, Cocoa Akure and Cocoa products, Ede Osun State.
>
> Within a period of 13 years, it had established strong relations with overseas cocoa product buyers such as Theobroma BV Netherlands; Euromar Berlin; Trading and Services France; Union Chocolate Poland; Delfi Cocoa (Europe) France/ Netherlands; Indcresa Spain; All trade international France.
>
> Solid relationships were also established with local users such as Nestle Nigeria Plc and Promasidor Nigeria Limited, makers of Cowbell Milk and Cocoa products.
>
> In March 2001, the company diversified into processing of palm kernel with the establishment of a 20,000 MT per annum crushing facility in Ibadan.
>
> The products which are mainly crude palm kernel oil and palm kernel cake are sold locally to industrial users such as edible oil refineries and soap manufacturers.

Our major customers in this business are Lina Oil Mills Ltd, Sudit Oil Mills Ltd, Alkanaah Industries Ltd all in Ibadan and Smooford Industries Ltd in Iperu, Ogun State. This facility is being forward integrated into Palm Kernel Oil Refinery with the acquisition of a 50,000 metric tons per annum vegetable oil refinery in Ibadan.

Over a period of 16 years, FTN Cocoa Processors Plc has processed about 64,000 MT of cocoa beans and 90,000 MT of palm kernel.

Our experience in cocoa processing business led to the informed decision to lease Cocoa Products Company Ltd, Ille-Oluji, Ondo State in 2003, at a time the company was moribund. Our successful turn-around of the company paved way for its privatization in 2006. In 2005, the company decided to venture into full scale self production. The process commenced in March 2006. The factory covers an area of approximately 4 acres with initial processing capacity of 10,000 MT of cocoa beans. It is a fully integrated factory with packing lines for cocoa liquor, cocoa butter, cocoa cake and cocoa powder plant. We commissioned the factory in November 2007. An additional 10,000 MT capacity per annum line was commissioned in September 2011 while the vegetable oil aspect was commissioned in January 2013.

If a single company can generate this huge impact, you can just imagine what will happen if more of such companies are established in different states of the country.

The results will be massive generation of employment; massive foreign exchange and massive export opportunities.

It is my belief that if we have more of these companies, then unemployment will be a thing of the past.

The future is very bright for agriculture in Nigeria if only we can have more of such companies in Nigeria in different states.

If we had more large farms operating at a higher capacity, poverty will not be a major issue in Nigeria anymore.

It is not only big farms that are making huge returns, even smaller farms are making lots of money. All things being equal, for a smallholder cocoa farm on 8 hectares of land, generating about 24 tons in a year and because they are hybrid seeds, after the second year, the farmer will have the first harvest which can be about 30% of what he has planted. Again, about the 4th year during which the farm will be at the highest capacity, it will be producing about 24tons and record about N16.8million annually – and that is assuming the lowest price of cocoa.

Bear in mind that this is the projected returns on an investment of about N5million.

The beauty of this is that as you await your windfall in the next three years, some plants can be planted alongside, like plantain which can be cultivated and harvested after 12 months.

Agriculture is a promising industry that I wish we can devote more attention to as a nation.

If investors are looking for where to invest their money, agriculture provides the opportunity for safe investment. Just take a look at the example I cited earlier on about cocoa farmers who see their investment yielding returns as the years go by.

Agriculture is one of the few investments you can commit N5million to and make about N16.8million annually. I don't know any other kind of investment that can give you such high returns if not agriculture.

Look at this calculation: N16.8million x 25 years = ASTONISHING!

As long as human beings exist, agricultural products will always be in high demand.

The part farmers need to focus on is the quality of seed and produce; because, produce will always be in high demand. In fact, some of these produce are in short supply and remain in high demand.

For example, the high cost of *garri* in the market is caused by the high demand for cassava which is now being used for other things like starch, flour, sweetener, etc.

Countries like Côte d'Ivoire are making a huge fortune from cocoa export. It is a major source of foreign exchange for them. Even countries like Cameroun and Ghana are not left out.

What Nigeria and other African nations need to work on is the processing of produce and packaging of products to meet international standards.

Now picture this: A gorgeously dressed man in an ultra-luxurious private jet en route the United Nations headquarters in New York to address world leaders. Now, that's the farmer of the future!

Chapter 2

CHAPTER 2
WHAT IS AGRICULTURAL BUSINESS?

The term *agricultural business* connotes business. Hence, it has to be treated as such and not as an activity. Business is about profit and loss. It is about transaction.

An agric business is constituted in order to promote products or services that add value and get reasonable value (compensation) in return. It also employs various organs in its operations like every other business (organs/arms such as marketing, accounting, systems, technology) for efficient delivery. It's subject to profit/loss, growth, expansion potential, etc., which is a function of the management style adopted.

The word business there means that you have to have in place everything that makes for a smooth business transaction. Things like packaging, inventory, business registration, cash inflows, outflows, inventory, business structure, marketing, customer segmentation, business plan, etc., must all be in place.

Agricultural business involves the strategic execution of operations and management of resources.

Also, because the success or failure of an agricultural business is determined by the same economic principles guiding other forms of business (e.g. factors such as exchange rate, inflation, government policies, etc.) proper forecast and projections are also essential.

> AGRIC BUSINESS SHOULD NOT BE TREATED PASSIVELY. BEING PASSIVE HAS MADE A LOT OF INVESTMENTS IN THE INDUSTRY GO DOWN THE DRAIN.

Training is required at all levels of operation. Agricultural business involvement can be in the form of partnership, sole proprietorship, investment, or limited liability. The choice of which structure to adopt is determined by vision, funds and knowledge of this business.

It is pertinent to note that an agricultural business will also go through the stages peculiar to other ventures. Stages like the Startup Phase, Stability Phase, Profit Making and Expansion Phase must be expected and adequately prepared for.

An agricultural business must be seen as an occupation. That is why for me, it is a fulltime job. The emphasis on *agricultural business* is very necessary to enlighten anyone coming into this business that it is a fulltime job and it has to be treated as such.

It has to be given the attention it deserves. You have to pay attention to details; you have to pay attention to figures, analysis, and projections.

You must know what you're doing because agricultural business is basically the business of generating maximum returns from investment and to make reasonable returns/income.

Agricultural business is not subsistence farming but an enterprise big enough to sustain itself and employ other people.

It should not be treated passively. Being passive has made a lot of investments in the industry go down the drain.

Not giving agricultural business active participation will result in loss of investment. It must be given the utmost attention. The right professionals should be engaged when you need them.

Myths about Agriculture
- *It is practiced only by the illiterate*

A lot of people have the wrong notion that it is only illiterate people that actively practice agriculture. I believe that is why a lot people shy away from the agricultural business hitherto, as they were not seeing the treasures loaded in the industry.

I am a testament to the fact that refined and educated people are in agriculture. I am a Geophysicist by training.

There are lawyers, engineers, and people with multiple degrees from leading universities around the world who are actively involved in this agriculture business with us.

Agriculture is practiced by enlightened and educated people. The wrong mindset of thinking it is for the illiterate has kept a lot of people from coming into the industry, though they remain enthralled by the pride, the glamour and razzmatazz they see in other professions.

My dear reader, let me emphasize: Farming business is not only for the uneducated. Illiterate people are limited in their capacity as to what to do and achieve - their minds cannot conceive much.

Of course, it would even shock you to know that there are some uneducated ones who are in this agricultural business and trading in millions of naira.

People need to face reality; because there are some of these illiterates that I know who are earning in excess of N60million from their farms annually. There are these so called illiterates buying cars every year from their farm sales. In contrast, some people with white collar jobs are struggling to pay their bills amounting to only a few thousands of Naira.

➤ *It is not lucrative; and all farmers are poor*

I think the local movies have contributed to this mindset. In such movies, farmers are depicted as poor and wretched! Mechanized farmers are rarely shown in local movies. The picture that the local movie producers use to harass the sights of their audiences is of farmers with hoes and cutlasses.

Also, I think this mindset has been fueled by what urban dwellers see while travelling outside town - in which farmers display their wares along the road and are desperately looking for buyers.

Farming is lucrative, if well managed. There are farms in Nigeria that are earning billions. That should be a pointer to you that the business of agriculture is lucrative. Except you can tell me millionaires are poor, it is only then that you can confidently say farmers are poor.

Tunde Banjoko

➤ *One has to relocate to the village and suffer*

The truth of the matter is that farming requires a lot of attention. So, it must be given its rightful attention.

The time you will commit to farming, however, will depend on the size of land and the crops you're cultivating; plus, of course, what portion of the agric business value-chain you have chosen to operate in.

If it is a vegetable or fruits farm you are cultivating, it can be done in the city because you don't need a large expanse of land for that. But if you are looking to cultivate a large expanse of land, it is practically impossible to acquire around 400 hectares of land for farming purposes in a metropolitan city like Lagos, for example. 400 hectares of land is about the size of a major town on its own.

There is a rice farm in Nassarawa State that covers about 43,000 hectares of land. Having that kind of large expanse of land in the city is not possible. One needs to move into the outskirts to get such a large expanse of land.

Now, even though operations take place in the village, those managing the farm don't necessary have to 'stay' in the village. There are farms in this country equipped with modern amenities like electricity, satellite decoders, noise proof generators, and any modern social amenities your mind can think of.

There are farms with staff houses. There are farms with good road networks. You will be amazed at the kind of facilities you will encounter in some farms which will make you to wonder if you are in the farm or in the city.

Farming in the village is not a ticket to suffering. Those of us who are farming are only operating in the village but do not live in the village. The village is just a base of operation.

Some farms have corporate head offices in major cities like Lagos, Abuja and Ibadan while farming operations go on in the village. It is much like owning an oil bloc: Exploration is done offshore. Those who explore offshore do not necessarily have to live offshore permanently.

And the people who own the oil bloc do not stay offshore. After exploration, they go to their respective bases. It is the same methodology in farming.

Farming has to be done where land is readily available. Farming cannot be successfully done in a congested city like Lagos. Even the cost of set up in Lagos will be very high. Farmers do not necessary stay in the village but farming takes place in the village. That clarity is needed.

> WHEN YOU START OUT AS AN APPRENTICE ON A FUNCTIONING FARM, YOU WILL SAVE YOURSELF TIME AND MONEY. YOU WILL BE GUIDED ON HOW YOU CAN START WITH LITTLE OR NO FUND.

➤ *One needs large capital to start or operate such a business*

A lot of people who show interest in agricultural business have this wrong notion that you need a huge sum of money to commence. Let me tell you that once the intention is there, several ways of starting without huge capital are available.

Farming is like every other business where you can start small and grow big. Once the determination is there, I believe getting the land and what to cultivate are secondary.

In some cases, you can start your career in agriculture as a volunteer in some other farms in order to learn the ropes before commencing your own business.

You really do not need large sums of money to start. Yes, when you start out, you may be the only one who handles all the operations and administration requirements of the farm. However, as times goes on, you will be able to hire qualified people to handle every aspect of your operations.

Also, when you start out as an apprentice on a functioning farm, you will save yourself time and money. You will be guided on how you can start with little or no fund.

➤ *One has to own a piece of land*

You don't have to own a piece of land to be a farmer. You can lease a piece of land. Many times, as long as you are not cultivating cash crops, a lot of communities are ready to lease a piece of land to you for about four to five years.

You do not necessarily have to own land. Some families can give you land for free for agricultural purposes for an agreed time frame and arrangement on profit sharing.

Different arrangements can be worked out. You can cultivate a land and share the proceeds with the owner of the land. In this kind of arrangement, the capital you need is for paying people to clear the land and do some work on the farm. So, you really do not have to own a piece land to start farming.

Even though as time progresses, according to your analysis and projections, you might need to own your own piece of land.

In essence, you can start without buying a piece of land in different ways like leasing of land or sharing of proceeds with landowner(s).

Others are:

- ***Inherited or family land***: You may consider using your family or inherited land lying fallow in your village to start your agricultural business.
- ***Your backyard***: Yes, you read that well. Your backyard can serve as a launching pad for you into agricultural business. The space in your backyard can be put to good use.

Instances abound of people who converted their swimming pools into fish ponds. There are people making money from the vegetables they are cultivating in their backyards with about half a plot of land and they are making between N10, 000 to N20, 000 every month.

You can start in your backyard and learn some things along the way.

There are also examples of those who have poultry farms in their backyards and are making money as well. Yet, there are others who use a small oven - about 2 by 2 meter square - and all they do is buy fish, smoke them and sell.

There are people who only buy pigs, dice and sell. They don't own a piggery pen.

Land is not necessarily synonymous with agricultural business.

➤ *One must have a background in agriculture, either formally or by upbringing*

I will use myself as an example here: I have never had a village experience in my life. I was born and bred in the city of Lagos. Yet, I have a big farm.

What am I referring to? You don't have to be born in the village before you participate actively in agricultural business. What you actually need is to be equipped with the right knowledge and connected to the right people with requisite knowledge when you are considering investing in agriculture.

Agriculture is a business that can be successfully learnt. You don't really have to grow up in the village. You don't need to study agriculture. You don't need a formal training - even though you need to equip yourself with the right trainings as time progresses.

➤ *Agriculture Is Not Tech-Driven*

Agriculture is a full-fledged business that can be IT driven. For example, these days, people use walkie-talkies on the farm. Solar energy is powering lots of farms in Nigeria. There are CCTV cameras installed in many farms.

With the aid of IT, you can be in the United States and monitor what is going on in your farm in Nigeria.

In greenhouse farming, for example, a lot of simulations are being done using technology. Farming is not a local operation anymore. It can be technologically driven.

As your business grows in the agricultural industry, a lot of your operations will be tech-driven. Processing becomes automated, your daily operations are automated, and even weeding is done with tech equipment nowadays.

If your farm is IT driven, there will be little human interference in your farm. A lot of monitoring can be done using apps and mobile devices.

These myths, as described above, are unfounded and should be discarded.

Tunde Banjoko

CHAPTER 3
WHY GO INTO AGRICULTURAL BUSINESS?

The country is currently going through economic challenges majorly because our imports have exceeded our exports. We have been importing things we can produce locally.

The demand for foreign imported products has weighed heavily on the naira, making it less valuable against the US dollars. And, we are not exporting at the rate at which we are importing.

The good news is that there are huge demands for our local products like cassava, cocoa, sheer butter, nuts, vegetables, etc., in the international market. It's high time we took advantage of this gap and turn around the economy of Nigeria. The only way to do that is to get a lot more people involved in agricultural business because the existing farmers and other players in the industry cannot meet up with the demand.

As a nation, we have been distracted by the earnings from crude oil. We have forgotten or failed to realize that from exporting agricultural produce from Nigeria, the country can earn a lot of foreign exchange and thereby stabilize our forex.

I believe that, as a nation, we should look at this area. We need to start producing products that are in high demand in other climes so as to earn enough foreign exchange.

Below are some of our comparative advantages to justify this position:

Large Population

Our population is an advantage. People need food. It follows therefore that our ever exploding population is a big market for agricultural produce.

It has been estimated by the United Nations that Nigeria will be the 3rd largest country in the world by 2050, with approximately 399million – 500million people.

With that population, it is expected that the country will overtake the United States to be the third largest population after China and India. Large population means more mouths to feed. Agriculturalists will surely make lots of money.

Other reasons for participating in agricultural business are:

Input, output and returns are predictable

All things being equal, in agriculture, you can make a reasonable prediction of your returns from your investments.

You can easily make projections into your earnings because the market is a bit stable.

Agric Business Can Fail!

Minimal start up investment required

Most times, when you look at the various options by which you can start your farm, the most important things seem to be your interest and willingness.

In truth, you don't need a big farm to start. There are places in Nigeria where you can be given a piece of land to cultivate and operate for a while. There are some NGOs facilitating this kind of arrangement for interested farmers.

In some places as well, you can be given land and returns will be shared. Your minimum startup capital will depend on the size you are cultivating per time.

> YOU CAN EVEN START YOUR FARMING BUSINESS WITH ZERO CAPITAL, IF YOU CAN DO THE MANUAL WORK ON YOUR OWN BY CLEARING THE LAND, PLANTING, WEEDING AND HARVESTING.

You can even start your farming business with zero capital, if you can do the manual work on your own by clearing the land, planting, weeding and harvesting.

In any case, you don't require a fortune to start. You can always work out the modalities for starting. You may not start with buying hybrid seedlings. You could buy the local ones because they are cheaper, and you can even get some local seedlings for free.

So, depending on how you want to go about it, you really do not need huge fortunes to start your operations.

Profession with continuous demand

One beauty of the agricultural business is the continuity it offers, unlike other industries that are subjected to several factors. In the oil and gas industry, for example, the breakthrough in the technology for alternatives to oil has made the global demand for oil to fall drastically.

But in agriculture, alternatives can't be found to food. There may be need to adjust production, but the fact is that our produce will always be in high demand because the only means of survival is eating. As long as the earth remains, the demand for agricultural produce will continue.

Agriculture is a profession with continuous demand as long as human and human activities exist.

CHAPTER 4
GUIDE TO AGRICULTURAL BUSINESS

To be properly guided as you invest in the industry, you need to understand your purpose and motivation for venturing into agriculture. Proper knowledge of these will guide you.

For instance, if you plan to cultivate crops in commercial quantity for the long term, then the first thing to consider is land acquisition.

A lot of people get it wrong from this very point. They acquire land in a wrong location. Take note of this: before you acquire a land, you must enquire about the area and the terrain in which you are acquiring the land.

THE MISFORTUNE AND LOSS THAT A LOT OF PEOPLE VENTURING INTO AGRICULTURE EXPERIENCE START FROM THE LAND ACQUISITION STAGE.

The misfortune and loss that a lot of people venturing into agriculture experience start from the land acquisition stage. They may acquire land in a community that is hostile to agricultural business. Or, they acquire land in a community where herdsmen are having a field day. Some acquire land in locations that are isolated or where they are just not welcome.

The isolation could be a situation in which there are no other farmers, or nobody is interacting with them because they are not wanted by the community.

A community may be hostile to a farmer for something as mundane as acquiring a large expanse of land, when the community is only used to cultivating on small portions of land.

> BEFORE YOU ACQUIRE A PIECE OF LAND, YOU NEED TO CONDUCT A FACT-FINDING EXERCISE. DO SOME INVESTIGATION, OR GO THROUGH AN EXISTING FARMER INTO THAT COMMUNITY.

In order to avert these challenges during land acquisition, I will suggest that you consider either going through a mediator or making further enquiries about the land you plan to acquire.

Before you acquire a piece of land, you need to conduct a fact-finding exercise. Do some investigation, or go through an existing farmer into that community.

Your land acquisition is your first and most crucial task.

A lot of farms have been abandoned by new entrants into this business because of the failure to get it right at the land acquisition stage. They acquire land in areas that are hostile, envious, and areas where they are seen as threats or oppressors.

Once you get it wrong from this very beginning, then your relationship with that community will be very difficult. Operating in that setting may be difficult and it may mean that you won't work at all on your farm.

After the acquisition of the land, you must devise ways to integrate yourself into the community and then figure out what crops to cultivate or livestock to raise.

My advice for new entrants into this business is to sit down and count the cost. New entrants must know that planting the best seeds alone is not enough, the right quantity is also important.

Another way new entrants get it wrong is in deciding the time of planting. There are different ways of cultivating – you can plant the same crop at the different times and just this decision will demand that you cultivate the crops differently. You must be properly guided on this as a new entrant. If you are not properly guided, then you will be doing the seemingly right thing at the wrong time and gradually you will be losing your investment, as returns will not come as expected.

Furthermore, your human relation skills must be excellent. In agricultural business, you're dealing majorly with human beings. In Nigeria, most of the people that would be working with you may not understand your language. As a Yoruba man, you may be working with about 40 Hausa men on your farm. You may probably be forced to rely on sign language to convey your messages and interact with them.

Everything will have to be done via sign language as you strive to get the work done on your farm.

From experience, most of the people in the host communities of farms are always lazy. Such an observation will necessitate that you will bring people in from outside the community – even far away from your ethnic group. This will bring with it a measure of language barrier. You must put in extra effort to communicate with these sets of people working on your farm. You must be patient. If you are unable to communicate very well, the job will be left undone or half-done.

In addition, your relationship with the host communities supersedes all the money you may have invested into your farm. You must be wary of driving your car past everybody on your way to your farm without greeting them. At times, you may have to spend quite some time chatting and socializing with them before going to your farm. These are some of the little things you must do to succeed in agriculture.

Please don't merely read what you find on the internet and start running with it. A lot of things are being posted online which are not verified or are not peculiar to our own environment.

As per your arithmetic and accounting knowledge, it should be fairly good because you will constantly be calculating your yield. You must know the cost of your inputs and outputs. You must also know precisely how much it is costing you to maintain your farm per time.

Your financial discipline also has to be topnotch, in order not to torpedo the business with indiscriminate withdrawals from your business account.

This brings me to the issue of cultivation.

The maintenance of your farm is very crucial. One advice I usually give farmers is this: even where you have 100 hectares available, if you can only maintain 50 hectares during cultivation period, then focus on that portion. Don't just venture into cultivating the whole 100 hectares at a go. It may be overwhelming for you. Again, if you get stuck while cultivating the whole 100 hectares, it could affect your entire investment.

I have noticed that a lot of people that are venturing for the first time into agriculture business are always excited about the number of hectares of land that they possess. But after planting, maintenance required to ensure a good yield becomes a big challenge and this will cause stagnation.

This situation will undoubtedly affect the projected returns of such a farm and may then becloud the judgment of such a person who will believe that agriculture is not a profitable venture.

You must always factor in the cost of maintaining your farm. In my opinion, this is more crucial than any other thing. You must learn to work in phases, if need be.

Business Structure Guide

As stated earlier, a functional agricultural business is like every other thriving business in town where you have all aspects of the business structure working optimally.

You don't have to start with all the professionals, as you can outsource some of your operations. At startup stage, you can have one person or two combining the job roles of an accountant, admin officer, HR, etc.

Agric Business Can Fail!

As you grow, the other departments become functional with qualified professionals manning operations and the erstwhile outsourced areas becoming fully functional in-house.

You can start your business as a sole proprietor but you don't have to remain at that level. Upgrade as you progress. There are farms with board members and foreign partners and even foreign offices.

You should be registered with the Corporate Affairs Commission (CAC) either from the beginning or as operation progresses. Register also with the Federal Inland Revenue Service (FIRS) for the purpose of paying your taxes and ensure that you audit your account regularly. And, ensure you have external auditors who come in regularly to crosscheck your figures.

The legal aspects of your business must be gotten right as well. Engage a lawyer to guide you through the legal landmines of your business.

Indeed, there is no limit to the structure you can have in an agricultural business. Your organogram can be compared to any business from around the world. Agriculture is a big business. As you grow, you can have various arms of your agricultural business.

For example, I started alone when I commenced business. No board. No partner. No worker. I was the only staff. I acquired 36 acres of land and started cultivating it bit by bit. I didn't have to put anyone on my payroll. What I did was to get people to do the clearing, planting, weeding and at intervals I was overseeing their activities.

As my operations grew, I had to start doing monthly and bimonthly crop production. I started cultivating vegetables and getting more staff on board. Then I got an accountant and about six staff working with me. After a year, I acquired additional 44 acres of land. With that size, I needed more people, so I employed people even as I outsourced some tasks to professionals.

From there, we moved into livestock production and we needed more hands. We got more people on board to oversee that part of the business.

Today, we have grown in assets and have reputable people on our board of directors. We have several skilled, unskilled and casual workers on our payroll.

> INDEED, THERE IS NO LIMIT TO THE STRUCTURE YOU CAN HAVE IN AN AGRICULTURAL BUSINESS. YOUR ORGANOGRAM CAN BE COMPARED TO ANY BUSINESS FROM AROUND THE WORLD.

When we started farm management consultancy, we got professionals. This arm of our business handles setting up of farms and other areas of business interest in the agriculture value chain for clients. This arm takes care of those interested in this industry but do not have the time and technical know-how to go about it.

We basically turn dreams and conceptualized ideas into reality. Further, we set up systems to keep the business running for the clients while under our management supervision for an agreed period of time. This is done to ensure maximum output and profitability.

Our activities involve the acquisition of required facility or land either on outright purchase or lease. We as well oversee operations from acquisition, planting, farm monitoring to harvesting and sales of produce.

Our management service is done in conjunction with several professionals and institutions to aid the best output.

Interested in this service? Get a free quote here: http://www.bofarmsltd.com/contact.php

Highlight of Factors to Consider Before Siting a Farm
- Availability of labor
- Understanding of the peculiar challenges confronting the community such as herdsmen invasion, erosion, etc.
- Accessibility of farm (Road networks)
- Presence of other farms or farmers

Tunde Banjoko

CHAPTER 5
BEFORE YOU QUIT YOUR JOB FOR AGRICULTURAL BUSINESS

Are you considering quitting your job and venturing into the agricultural business straightaway? Wait! Don't take that plunge yet.

Yes, I know that the projected returns in the agricultural business is somewhat tempting but you need to count the cost if you are planning to make a career switch into the agricultural industry.

Before taking the leap, there are some questions you must answer. One of them is that you must clarify your motive for coming into the industry.

Certainly, your motive has to be right. Quick money mentality will make you lose your investment quickly.

If you are planning to invest in this industry, you must understand timing and other factors that humans have no control over. You must also understand the timing of returns on your investment.

It is imperative that you have a proper perspective on whether you're expecting the projected income from the agricultural business to replace your monthly paycheck from your present job or expecting quarterly returns.

To successfully transit from your present employment into the agricultural business, you must also ask yourself the following questions and emerge with satisfactory answers:

Will you consider setting up your farm now, run it on a part-time basis and expect returns in the next four years – when you can now confidently resign and come on board fully? At that time, your investments might have matured to the extent that your returns from the business will be the same as or even more than your annual income in your present job

Is your motive just to have a passive source of income without resigning your present job?

Answer these questions properly, and then can you be well advised on how to proceed.

These answers will guide you as to where to invest in the industry and will also determine the cost of input.

QUICK MONEY MENTALITY WILL MAKE YOU LOSE YOUR INVESTMENT QUICKLY.

Monthly & Bi-Weekly Revenue

After satisfactory answers to your motive, the next step is about what kind of set up you are looking to put together/build.

There are various options to consider. Please note that agriculture is not by size but by effective management. So, for somebody who is looking at monthly or bi-weekly returns, the best option is the cultivation of vegetables.

If you are cultivating vegetables, you need to take a decision on whether to go for Green House or Open Farming.

In my opinion, standard Green House farming will give you the best returns.

Green House farming technique is a modern way of farming where your crops are enclosed and the inputs are well regulated.

In Green House, sunlight, water, fertilizer, atmosphere, temperature, etc., can be measured and adequately controlled; unlike the open farm where you don't have control over the amount of rainfall, sunshine, etc.

Unlike in the open farm where crops are not effectively shielded from parasites, animals, invaders, etc., in a Green House farming set up, crops are properly shielded from the weather and animals.

Though setting up is a bit costly; once you can put together the cost of setting it up, it can be the best type of farming especially for vegetable farming.

The size of the farm is almost irrelevant as a Green House farm can be set up on a small space of land.

Another option is Aquaponics Farming. This type of farming is done in areas where there is almost no land. So planting on waters will be the option here.

In this part of Africa, it is not popular because we are a continent blessed with large expanses of land. These forms of farming are especially for farmers that are into the cultivation of vegetables and fruits. However, for cash crops and others, it has to be in the open farm on large hectares of land.

To round off our discussion on monthly returns, please note that it will be a mistake to invest in cash crops if you're expecting monthly income because it could take up to three years before you start reaping your investment.

Annual Returns

For those who are not really after the monthly return but looking for annual returns, you can consider crops like Cassava, Yam, Plantain, etc.

For those who have the future in mind, like 3 years and upward, you may consider cash crops.

Entry Strategy

Those desirous of investing in the agricultural business can come in through the following ways:

Own a share in an existing farm: One of the fastest ways of entry into the industry is to look for an existing and thriving farm that is open for investment and own a share therein.

> AGRICULTURAL BUSINESS IS BEYOND A BUSINESS PLAN; BECAUSE YOU ARE DEALING WITH ELEMENTS THAT ARE BEYOND HUMAN BEINGS LIKE SUN, RAIN, ANIMALS, HUMAN BEINGS, INFRASTRUCTURE DEFICIT, UNSKILLED LABOR FORCE, ETC.

This is a less risky option for professionals in other sectors who are considering making a switch into the agricultural industry or seeking a form of stable investment.

You can approach an existing farm and if they are willing, you agree on a certain percentage and then you become a part-owner.

With this option, you don't have to bother much with so many intricacies of agriculture, since you're investing in an existing and thriving farm that has knowledgeable personnel and management at the helm of affairs.

Yours will be to inject funds and maybe expertise and own a part of the farm.

So, instead of setting up from scratch, you buy shares. It is somewhat safe for a professional in another sector who doesn't want to go through the rigors of starting from the very beginning.

100% ownership of farm under a Farm Management Company: This is a situation where you own the farm 100% but it is placed under a farm management company.

Here, you are expected to fund the operations of the farm 100% while the management company oversees the farm for you. Hence, you are saved from the hassles of the day-to-day management of the farm. That burden belongs to the farm management company. They will mentor and hold your hand to wade through the booby traps inherent in the business.

100% ownership from scratch: Here, you dive headlong into the pool of agricultural business with or without the supervision of a farm management company or partnership with an existing farm.

You will start from the scratch and own your investment 100%. This allows you full control over your investment. The danger in this route is that you will learn by trial-and-error which may be costly. You may lose all or part of your investment if you are not careful and because of lack of knowledge.

You will be confronted with lots of realities that will shock or surprise you. For instance, you might be shocked that the day you want to harvest perishable products, no one will show up to work on your farm. You might be surprised that your off-takers will fail to show up to buy your perishable products, or at what your suppliers will do to you. Let's not even describe what animals can (innocently) do to investments on your farm.

Agricultural business is beyond a business plan; because you are dealing with elements that are beyond human beings like sun, rain, animals, human beings, infrastructure deficit, unskilled labor force, etc.

Agricultural business is what you roll up your sleeves and get fully engaged in. And, of course, you can pool resources with other experts to share the burden with you.

If you are not ready to go through the stress of dealing with illiterates and unskilled labor force, then you are safer pitching your tent with a farm management company or partnering with an existing farm.

At BO Farms Ltd, we help new entrants into the agricultural business to manage their farms. We take the burden off you and do the day-to-day management of your farm. Please visit our website (www.bofarmsltd.com) for more details.

Hands-on Knowledge vs. Theory!

Reading books on agriculture is good but that is not enough. Listening to lectures on agriculture or attending agriculture seminars is good but that is not enough to give you a fortune in the industry.

The best way to succeed in this industry is to ask the right questions from those that are actively involved in the agricultural business - and not from those who aren't active farmers or active players in the agricultural industry.

> IT IS FUNNY AND SOMEWHAT IRONIC THAT SOME PEOPLE WHO HAVE NEVER OWNED A PLOT OF FARMLAND OR DONE ANYTHING IN THE INDUSTRY WOULD BE LECTURING PEOPLE ON THE BUSINESS OF FARMING.

It is funny and somewhat ironic that some people who have never owned a plot of farmland or done anything in the industry would be lecturing people on the business of farming. Their knowledge is at best academic exercise with no connection to reality.

A lot of the information this theorists dish out are not true. They throw out outrageous facts and figures on the returns to expect when investing in agriculture.

Therefore, it is safe for you to get your enquiries from true farmers who are in the 'trenches' and not armchair agriculture analysts parading themselves as experts.

You can read materials on farming from reliable and known sources. However, don't base your decisions only on what you have read. Let your reading be a guide to make further enquiries and on-the-spot assessments.

I have seen situations where some of these analysts would give all kinds of data and on further probe, it would be discovered that they are bogus.

I will therefore advise new entrants into the industry to make enquiries from existing farmers. Existing farmers will tell you the pros and the cons of your intended actions and plans.

They can tell you where they have failed and succeeded. They can tell you what they have done that didn't go well and how to avoid that mistake. They will inform you about how they eventually got it right.

Agric Business Can Fail!

CHAPTER 6
STRUCTURE & STAGES OF AGRICULTURAL BUSINESS

In terms of structure and stages of the business of agriculture, no noticeable difference exists between this and what is obtainable in other professions and industries.

The option you will embrace will be determined by the vision you have for your company and the knowledge of the industry. This will then determine where and how you play in the industry.

Also, the funds available at your disposal can also be a determining factor of the kind of business you will incorporate.

As stated above, your knowledge of the industry will determine where you play in the industry. If your knowledge is limited, you can be an investor and sit on the board to have a say in the running of the business.

The following are the possible structure options that you may adopt as you set up your agricultural business:

Sole Proprietorship – A sole proprietor is the most basic type of business structure you may decide to adopt. You alone will be responsible for the profit and loss of the company.

You alone will also be responsible for the assets and liabilities of the company. You, as an individual, are not distinct from the business.

One of the advantages of being a sole proprietor is that your startup capital is low. Also, there are limited legal hurdles to cross when setting up as a sole proprietor.

On the other hand, one of the major disadvantages is that you have unlimited liability for debts, as there's no legal distinction between private and business assets.

Finally, the scale of operations may be too high for you alone to handle.

Partnership- You can make an entry into the industry as an investor. Here you invest into an existing farm that you are sure of their operations, management and business model or partnership formed by a group of people bringing in their different skills and resource together to own and run a farm.

There are different types of partnerships, which depend on the nature of the arrangement and partner responsibility for the daily management of the business.

Ensure you consult your attorney when considering partnership as an option.

Limited Liability Company – With a limited liability company (LLC), the owners of the company cannot be held personally liable for the company's debts or liabilities unlike what is obtainable in a sole proprietorship structure.

Cooperative – You can join other like minds to pool resources together to meet a collective need.

> AT THE STARTUP PHASE, YOU ARE BOUND TO MAKE MANY ERRORS, ESPECIALLY BECAUSE YOU ARE LIKELY TO BE MEETING A LOT OF CHALLENGES FOR THE FIRST TIME.

STAGES OF THE BUSINESS

No matter the structure of business you decide to adopt, you will go through some phases which can span different numbers of years, depending on how fast you learn and adopt.

Your knowledge and inputs into the business will go a long way to determine how long you stay on a particular phase of your business.

The following are the stages every business owner in the industry will pass through:

The Start Up– This phase begins about the time you are acquiring the facilities, registering the business, setting up the farm, clearing and other activities you embark on to kick-start the farm.

The startup stage also covers your first, second and probably third production cycles which I am certain you will learn from.

You will learn a lot from how you went about your first operations - the clearing, weeding, planting, harvesting, marketing, etc. You will learn a lot while executing this first phase.

At the startup phase, you are bound to make many errors, especially because you are likely to be meeting a lot of challenges for the first time.

Errors are bound to happen. Unfortunately, it is at this phase that a lot of people quit because things are not working the way they envisaged in their analysis, projections and business plans.

I believe that the startup phase is the learning phase where you put to test your knowledge. It is a phase where you will test all that you think you know and quickly discard the half-knowledge you may possess.

For example, sometime ago I saw an erroneous publication on the internet as it relates to the cultivation of plantain. The author of the publication falsely claimed that plantain cultivation can be done within six months and it will be ready for harvest within that period; whereas, plantain cultivation can take up to 12months or a little more. Even though the harvest can be fast-tracked to about 8 months with fertilizer, experience has shown that the market may reject it.

The overall feedback from the local market is not always good if fertilizer is applied to alter plantain's natural cycle. A lot of traders don't like heavy fertilizer-grown plantain. They prefer to buy unripe plantain and keep it for like a week in order to boil, roast or process it into plantain flour.

They wouldn't appreciate a situation where they can't store for a long period before it gets spoilt. If they are buying unripe, they want it to last for three to five days. The ones that are fertilizer produced will not enjoy continuous patronage in the market.

This is an example of what you will learn at the startup stage. The startup phase is a test phase. You should not be in hurry.

Don't quit because of momentary challenges. So many people back out at this stage because they feel agro-business is not profitable against their expectation.

Stability Phase- At this stage, you have learnt your lessons. You know who to speak to and who to approach for answers to issues.

At this stage, you are no longer working with other people's experience. You are working with your own personal experience.

At this stage also, your predictions and projections are somewhat accurate. You have good rapport with your stakeholders, the market, etc. And you have wider knowledge of the market, too.

Another characteristic of this phase is that your loss is minimal because of the knowledge and experience you have garnered thus far.

Expansion Stage– The expansion stage is where you increase production for more profitability.

At this stage, you will bring to bear what you have learned and understood about the business at the startup and stability phases.

At the start up stage, you may have made some losses. And, at the stability stage, your losses will very likely have been minimized. Therefore, at the expansion stage, you can easily expect profits because trial-and-error would have been greatly minimized.

Please note that if you are coming into this industry, you need to be patient. There is no absolute timeline for each of these stages highlighted above.

Depending on how you learn and how you respond to the dynamics of the market, you could spend months or years in each of the stages.

THE BUSINESS IN THE VALUE CHAIN

Boundless opportunities exist in the agricultural industry. Hence, as a new entrant into the industry, there is enough room for you to invest and make substantial returns on your investment.

Your responsibility as an existing or a new entry into this industry is to identify a gap or need and move in swiftly to create value. Not everyone can be on the farm cultivating crops or rearing animals.

We should look at different value chains so that the overall effects will be good for our economy and we can gain more.

When considering the different areas where you can add value, put into consideration your passion, hobby, skills, resources, and relationships.

Here are some of the value chains in the industry:

Production - Crops & Rearing of Animals

The primary area of agriculture is the production of crops and rearing of animals. It is these which demand operation on land or facilities for the purpose of producing crops like maize, plantain, cocoa, etc.

This aspect is good and the returns good as well. Once you know how to go about it - acquiring the land, maintaining the farm, and knowing where and when to sell your produce - this aspect can be considered, if you have the passion and if you don't mind interacting with people in the villages and people from other neighboring African countries.

Agric Business Can Fail!

Processing

Close to production is the processing of what has been produced by the farmers. This involves using automated equipment, locally fabricated equipment or imported equipment to turn some of these locally produced crops/materials into finished goods.

For example, there are locally-made machines used in producing fresh fruit juice. There are people who use automated machines to produce *garri* and even to kill animals - from killing to dissecting of the animals into various parts and packaging into polythene nylons.

> PROCESSING IS A BIG DEAL. IT IS A FULL-FLEDGED OPERATION ON ITS OWN. THOSE WHO GET ENGAGED IN THIS DO NOT HAVE TO OWN A FARM. IT IS VERY LUCRATIVE IF YOU HAVE ALL THAT IT TAKES TO START A PROCESSING BUSINESS.

Processing is a big deal. It is a full-fledged operation on its own. Those who get engaged in this do not have to own a farm. It is very lucrative if you have all that it takes to start a processing business.

For example, it takes 12 months for a farmer to grow and harvest cassava. Recall that in Chapter 1 of this book, I revealed that a farmer can spend about N932, 000 to produce cassava on 8 Hectares of land and after selling in 12 months' time, he gets about N2.4 Million. At the end of the transaction period, he would have made about 157.5% returns on his investment.

But for a processor, that same volume of cassava when processed into *garri* can earn him about N7million. That's about 191.67% in two weeks, if he buys his cassava from the farmer referred to above. If, however, he owns the farm and made the initial investment of N932, 000, his return on investment will amount to a whopping 651.07%, though the transaction period is longer. That's the beauty of processing agricultural products.

Processing is a major challenge in Nigeria and the whole of Africa. Many of the things we produce are not processed. We have shrewd foreigners who export the raw materials and import to us the finished products at ten times the price of the raw materials.

Our cocoa is exported to advanced nations where it is processed into chocolates and beverages.

The chocolates and beverages are then imported into Nigeria and other African countries at a cost far higher than the cocoa which produced it was sold for.

In 2014, CNN aired a special edition of Quest Means Business. On the show, it was a pity to behold how farmers who had been cultivating cocoa for decades have never tasted a chocolate in their whole lives.

Research has shown that where a cocoa farmer makes N2billion from production, the processor must have made about N18billion as a result of taking the time to process it into another form, simply put value addition.

Processing for those who can afford the processing plant is a major investment. We have not really harnessed it in Nigeria, and that is why many of our farm produce are wasting away.

It is a sad commentary that people are still exporting some of our local produce and then bringing back the processed goods at a higher price. This is one of the reasons it could look like farming is not lucrative. It is why we sometimes have gluts in agricultural production.

If we had enough processing plants, you will realize that we have not started producing enough as a nation; even though we have the wrong notion that we are over-producing.

This notion of course is fueled by the fact that a lot of our produce are wasting away in the absence of processing.

Our challenge is not with production but with processing. Sufficient processing is not taking place around the African continent.

As you know, every challenge presents an opportunity. Hence, as a result of reading this book, you may decide to set up a processing plant. In essence, you don't necessarily have to own a farm. You only need to mop-up produce from various farmers to process and sell back into the market and you will make substantial profit.

Storage

Closely related to the discussion about processing is storage facilities. Both the raw farm produce and processed products require storage facilities.

You may choose not to be a primary producer or a processor. Rather, you could decide to only provide storage facilities. By so doing, you would have closed a huge gap that ordinarily would translate to wastage. Thereby, you would increase the value of what is being produced.

The lifespan of some of our farm produce could be extended to up to six months, a year or more than that, if we get the right storage. You may not be aware but some of the goods imported into the country are more than eight years old in the countries where they originate from.

When we import, we stand a higher chance of buying goods that are close to their expiry dates as a nation. We need companies that can set up storage facilities across the country. True, there are few of them existing at the moment, but we need more.

The traditional means of storing our grains and other produce are no longer sustainable. We need to look at modern ways of storage like the cocoons, silos, etc.

Food technology professionals should look into this area, proffer sustainable solutions and make them available commercially.

In Nigeria, most crops aren't available all year round but they can be preserved all year round. Plantain can be preserved for four to six months, i.e. stored during the period of bumper harvest and made available during off-season, so we can have it all year round. We should look into all these techniques and technologies on how storage and preservation can be done and get people involved in the value chain.

Transportation

An area of investment also available is transportation of farm produce from the farm to the market.

The transportation of both the primary and finished products is a major constrain to farmers in Nigeria.

Most of the farms in Nigeria today are not very motorable. You may have a large expanse of land with bumper harvest but without a good road network, transporting your goods will be a major challenge; because a lot of trucks get trapped on bad roads, especially during the rainy season.

Imagine harvesting plantain on such a farm and the truck transporting it to the market gets stuck for up to four days? The situation can only lead to a major loss of revenue.

Modern tractors, good trucks for transporting products out and cooling vans are much needed in the industry.

The industry needs people who can provide cooling vans to prevent some of these products from rotting.

There are many products produced in the northern part of Nigeria, for example, which are in high demand in the southern part of Nigeria. However, due to lack of adequate transportation, they are not readily available there.

Logistics professionals can come into the industry and resolve these highlighted issues.

Marketing

After getting the goods produced, stored, processed and transported to the right location, marketing of these products is a major issue for some farmers, hence the need for adequate attention and knowledge.

The agricultural industry needs people who can network the primary producers with companies who are in need of farm produce. At times, some goods are being produced but getting people to off-take them becomes a big challenge.

Professionals who have strength in marketing can come into the industry and just work as middlemen to connect the primary producers with the companies or countries that require the products.

The commission you earn can be a source of passive income for you, if you are considering entering into this industry as a marketer while still keeping your day job.

Marketers and Business Development professionals are needed in the industry. Professionals who can network and close the gap between the producers, processors, industries and countries that need this produce are in high demand.

Export

Exporting of agricultural produce is another terrain you may consider playing in. You must, however, understand what the individual requirements are to export some of these agricultural products.

Cocoa when exported, for example, is rarely exported by the same person who produced it.

People with the knowledge and experience in shipping can look into shipping of agricultural produce to those countries where they are in high demand.

Those who know about the documentation required, as well as how to access the funds available to encourage shipping, should come into the industry. Many times, farmers either cannot afford the cost of shipping or do not know about the intricacies of the shipping industry.

If you have the funds, access to networks and the technical know-how of port operations, I am of the opinion that exporting agriculture products will be a good investment for you.

This will also help to mop-up the excesses on ground and earn the nation the much-needed foreign exchange.

Tunde Banjoko

CHAPTER 7
SOURCES OF CAPITAL

Agricultural business can be capital intensive if you are going full-scale. It is however advisable to start small and grow big. When you start small, you won't put your investment too much at risk.

You will learn a lot at the startup stage, then leverage the experience you have garnered to move through the other stages as outlined in Chapter 6.

At every stage of your business, money is needed. This is how you can source for funds:

Family and Friends

You can start your farm by raising funds from families and friends. When lending from families and friends, I will advise that the payment structure should be annual not monthly.

You need to make family and friends know the gestation period of what you are putting their money into, so that expectations about refund are well managed tied to at the harvest or production cycle, and not earlier.

This would give you rest of mind, since they know what you are doing.

If you are getting money from families and friends, it is good to carry them along every step of the way, so that they know when they will be getting their money back.

> IT IS ADVISABLE TO START SMALL AND GROW BIG. WHEN YOU START SMALL, YOU WON'T PUT YOUR INVESTMENT TOO MUCH AT RISK.

Another strategy to source for funds from families and friends is to promise them a certain percentage of profits at the end of harvesting and marketing referred to as a profit-sharing arrangement.

You will make them pool resources together, go into a joint venture agreement and then declare dividends at the end of the farming cycle.

Banks

Funds earmarked for agricultural purposes are also available from the following banks in Nigeria: Commercial Banks; Microfinance Banks; Bank of Agriculture; Bank of Industry, etc.

You can walk into any commercial bank and request to know about their agriculture finance package.

Some Microfinance banks across the country specifically fund agro-business. Their terms vary depending on the size of the loan requested.

o   *Bank of Agriculture*

It is a federal government-owned development bank with a mandate to provide low cost credit to small holder and commercial farmers, and small and medium scale rural enterprises. It also provides micro financing to small and medium scale non-agricultural enterprises.

The bank's key mandates include:

- Provision of credit to support all activities in the Agricultural Value Chain
- Provision of non-agricultural micro credit to the poor segment of the society, comprising rural artisans, petty traders, etc.
- Capacity development for the promotion of co-operatives and agricultural information systems.
- Provision of technical support and extension services
- Boosting of opportunities for self-employment in the rural areas to stem rural-urban migration.

- Inculcation of banking habits at the grass-roots of the Nigerian society.

As an individual, you can get up to N250, 000 from the Bank of Agriculture. They usually advise people to come together in co-operatives. And, if you are collecting so much, you will be required to bring a surety and collateral, too.

You may contact the bank at: http://www.boanig.com/contact

   o   **Bank of Industry (BOI)**

The Bank of Industry Limited (BOI) is Nigeria's oldest, largest and most successful development financing institution.

Its mandate is to provide financial assistance for the establishment of large, medium and small projects, as well as the expansion, diversification and modernization of existing enterprises; and rehabilitation of existing ones.

The bank also intervenes in the agricultural industry. Here are some of the interventions as contained on its website:

- ***Cassava Bread Development Fund:*** The Cassava Bread Development Fund was created by the Federal Government as part of the transformation policy in the agribusiness sector.

To ensure that Nigeria becomes the largest cassava processor, having occupied the position of largest producer of the commodity in the world, and guarantee the reduction of food import bills; a number of measures, including the cassava bread policy, were endorsed by the Government.

Government's intervention in the Cassava Value Chain by funding Cassava Processors and Bakers would translate to foreign exchange savings and job creation along the cassava value chain and also prevent post-harvest losses.

Target Market

The initiative is aimed at providing equipment and working capital support to Master Bakers and High Quality Cassava Flour (HQCF) processors across Nigeria.

The Cassava Bread Development Fund is aimed at the gradual substitution of wheat flour with cassava flour up to 20%.

Projected Impact

This initiative would translate to foreign exchange savings and job creation along the cassava value chain and also prevent post-harvest losses.

- <u>**National Programme on Food Security (NPFS):**</u> The implementing agencies for the scheme are the Federal Ministry of Agriculture and Rural Development (through the National Programme on Food Security (NPFS)) and the Bank of Industry (BOI) Limited.

The Memorandum of Understanding (MOU) designates BOI as the Fund Custodian and Administrator. BOI has the responsibility of fund disbursement, implementing and monitoring the projects, as well as recovering the loan and interest therefrom.

Target Market
- Agro-allied processors
- Farmers

Projected Impact

To enhance the productivity of the Apex Farmers Association (AFA), registered co-operative groups and SMEs in all thirty-six (36) States.

- <u>*Rice Intervention Fund:*</u> BOI is the designated fund manager of the N13.6billion Rice and

Cassava fund based on the MOU executed by the Federal Ministry of Agriculture and Rural Development (FMARD) and the Bank of Industry on October 23, 2014.

The Fund, which has defined hallmarks, has to be utilized solely for the establishment of ten (10) medium-scale Rice Mills of about 36,000 metric tons of paddy per annum and six (6) High Quality Cassava Flour Mills of about 18,000 metric tons of cassava tubers per annum capacity in identified locations across the nation, namely Kano, Kogi, Kebbi, Zamfara, Bayelsa, Bauchi, Benue, Ogun and Anambra States for the Rice Mills and in Ondo, Ogun, Abia, Delta, Nasarawa and Cross River States for the High Quality Cassava Flour Mills.

The Fund, which is close-ended, is limited to only applicants who have met all the laid down guidelines and recommended through competitive processes.

Target Market

The Fund will be accessed by Limited Liability Companies and Enterprises engaged in adding value to the rice/cassava commodities through the setting up of milling facilities.

- ***Sugar Development Council Fund:*** The Federal Government, in furtherance of its policy on Sugar development, instituted the National Sugar Development Council (NSDC) Fund for the establishment and resuscitation of companies engaged in the production of sugar, ethanol and sugar cane. The MOU between BOI and the National Sugar Development Council was signed on November 6, 2009.

The Fund was established to support the development of the value chain through local inclusion to reduce the nation's dependency on imported refined sugar.

Target Market

The Fund will be accessed by Limited Liability Companies and Enterprises engaged in sugar value chain such as Sugar plants, Sugar Refineries

- *Agro-Mechanization:* Agro Mechanization is the process of using agricultural machinery to mechanize the work of agriculture, thereby greatly increasing farm and farm worker productivity.

The target beneficiaries of this Product Program are;

- Those entities that will render agro-mechanisation services to the rural farmers.
- Established Farmers who want to acquire agro equipment for use in their farms.

Facility Type(s)

    a) Medium Term Loan
    b) Short Term Loan (where applicable)

Program Limit

The Scheme shall be wholly financed by Bank of Industry (BOI) with an initial seed fund of N10 Billion which will be allotted as follows:

- **Micro:** N3 Billion
- **Small:** N3 Billion
- **Medium:** N4 Billion

Each borrower category will be monitored independently by Required Minimum Distribution (RMD).

- ***Cottage Agro-Processors (CAP) Fund:***
BOI is establishing a Cottage Agro-Processors (CAP) Fund to support the establishment of cottage agro processing plants that will produce food products and raw materials for industries within and outside the Staple Crop Processing Zones (SCPZs) across Nigeria

The Fund will be accessed by Limited Liability Companies, Enterprises and Cooperative Societies engaged in the processing of agricultural products either into finished food products, as raw materials for industry or for the export market.

To apply for any of the itemized loans, please go to: http://www.boi.ng/apply/

Note: Most of these sources of funding provided by BOI and Bank of Agriculture are bogged down by unnecessary bureaucracy and politics.

If you can withstand the pressure, politicking, bureaucracy, red tapes, etc., then you can seek for funding from these government-established banks. Otherwise resort to your savings or money from family and friends.

Chapter 8

CHAPTER 8
COMMUNITY RELATIONS & PROFITABILITY

A strained relationship with your host community could spell doom for your investment, especially if you have invested in crop production and animal husbandry.

To get community relations right, investing in a community that is receptive to agricultural business is the first step. Thereafter, you must consciously initiate and maintain a strong and flourishing relationship with not only the leaders but the people of the community.

Your relationship and engagement with the youths and other interest groups in the community must be cordial.

To successfully engage your host community:

Employ Them

When you employ members of the community, you are taking one of the fastest routes of implanting yourself into their habitat.

In truth, employing some of the members of your host community into your organization is not based on their skills or industry but rather a public relations tool to integrate into that system.

If you need to engage 13 people for a task on your farm, I will advise that you hire about 3 or 4 from the village and hire others from outside. Those you employed from the community are there to complement most times and not to do the main job.

> EMPLOYING SOME OF THE MEMBERS OF YOUR HOST COMMUNITY INTO YOUR ORGANIZATION IS NOT BASED ON THEIR SKILLS OR INDUSTRY BUT RATHER A PUBLIC RELATIONS TOOL TO INTEGRATE INTO THAT SYSTEM.

It is a Community Social Responsibility (CSR) technique so that the members of the community won't complain that you bring people from outside to work in roles community members can perform.

Bear in mind that the output of three people you employ from the community may be the equivalent of one person's output hired from outside the community.

Nonetheless, simply because the indigenes are working on your farm and you are interacting with them, you're likely to get useful and lifesaving information from them.

You will be informed as to when to go out and come in. They will educate you about the hotspots in the community and serve as intelligence-gathering officers for you. They will also serve as unpaid security officers for your farm.

Their motivation to watch over your farm stems from the fact that they know that their daily bread is coming from your farm.

Socialize with them

Get involved in the host community's social life. Please note that I am not advocating that you join them to worship their idols/or necessarily adopt their religious beliefs. Socializing with them can be as simple as attending their weddings, naming ceremonies, funeral activities, school inter-house sports competitions, etc.

If physically you can't be at these social events, your cash will go a long way to communicate your loyalty. This will create acceptability and record relationship mileage for you.

In addition, you must know that driving through the village always without acknowledging cheers or greeting the villagers will land you in trouble. Once in a while alight from the vehicle and greet them if need be.

If you have something edible in your car, bring it out, sit and eat with them. If you're driving into the community and you see some of them roasting corn, for example, alight from your vehicle and eat with them. This has a way of making your bond with them even stronger; because eating with them has a way of making them see you as one of them.

Your success is very much tied to how amicably you relate with the community. I have seen cases where members of the community set a whole farm ablaze because of jealousy or perceived arrogance on the part of the farm owner.

Construct or Renovate Facilities/Amenities

You can also have the community on your side by embarking on projects that make life comfortable for them. If you have the resources, provide motorable roads within the community (this can be graded, not necessarily tarred), sink a borehole, etc.

If you can't afford that, consider renovating a few blocks of classrooms in a rundown school in the village. You may also consider providing drugs and other necessities for their health centers.

Know the Powerbrokers

Community relation is not complete without knowing and having the buy-in of the powerbrokers in your host community. The major stakeholders, thought leaders, opinion shapers and influencers in the community must be mapped out, identified and sufficiently acknowledged.

You must know your way around the community. You must also quickly befriend strategic people who wield enormous influence within the community to the extent that, one phone call to them can calm any storm raging in your direction.

It is not enough to merely know these leaders in the community; you must have a personal relationship with them. Have it in mind that when speaking to members of the community, you must be strategic with your words. Know their dos and don'ts in order not to run afoul of their customs and traditions.

The elders in the community can also serve as an 'advisory team' to you in the process of executing your plan. Some of them were involved in the agricultural business in time past, albeit in traditional format and as such, have rich experiences you can draw on.

They can advise you on which project to execute in a particular site. They can also advise you on timing. Some of them can guide you based on their historical and natural knowledge of the business.

Accordingly, your relationship with the community has a multiplier positive effect. Your staff are free and safe. If the community love you, invariably, it will rub off on your staff and investments in your farm.

Sell Cheaper to them

You need to strategically provide an opportunity for the members of your farm's host community to buy your farm produce at a cheaper price. This will endear you to their heart.

Before You Invest!

Warning! Before you invest in any community, please find out how receptive they are to visitors and agricultural business and understand the scope of work you are embarking on.

If you acquire a piece of land before making this enquiry, you have missed one of the most important parts of your business.

There are different ways you can gather information. Going through an existing farmer in the community will not only help with information gathering, it will help your integration into the community when you're satisfied with the information you have.

If you fail to get information from a farmer who is already doing business in the community, you may find yourself in a situation wherein you would be told that the piece of land you have acquired belongs to their gods and you can't farm on such land.

Not only that, you may find yourself entangled in a legal tussle over the piece of land you have already paid for.

PRODUCTIVITY, PROFITABILITY & MARKETING

From my experience in this industry, I can confidently postulate that the management of a farm is of greater importance than the size of the land.

One of the major reasons farmlands are abandoned is because people get stuck in the middle of operation. If a farmer requires N2million to cultivate for the season and what he has is N600, 000, if he can't raise the remaining funds on time, he will start counting loses from that point onward.

> FROM MY EXPERIENCE IN THIS INDUSTRY, I CAN CONFIDENTLY POSTULATE THAT THE MANAGEMENT OF A FARM IS OF GREATER IMPORTANCE THAN THE SIZE OF THE LAND.

When it is time for harvest and you have little or no money to harvest, some products begins to deteriorate. One good example of this is cassava. If some cassava specie is not harvested on time, it will start deteriorating.

Pathetically, your investment for 7-8 months can go completely into the drains just because you have no money to harvest or process as at when due.

That is why I pity those whose only boast is about the number of hectares of farmland they have acquired. The question they need to ask themselves is whether they can handle that level of operation.

As you consider acquiring land and cultivating, you must cultivate the portion of land you can maintain all through the farming cycle.

You can acquire as much land as you want but you have to cultivate on a portion you can manage per time. Once you start operation, you must consider your overall operation costs.

Your operation costs may include mental, physical, supervision and of course finance.

Productivity

Knowing the particular time of the year to plant seeds is one of the ways to ensure productivity.

The way some crops are planted in the rainy season is not the same during the dry season.

You must know how to go about planting at any time of the year. You must consider soil texture, and try to get the best of seeds to plant. There are some seeds that they die in the soil *after* they are planted.

Endeavour to get the best of seedlings from the right source, if you want to avoid your seeds dying in the soil.

Marketing

A lot of farmers fail at this point. The lack of marketing skills have left a lot of farmers in penury.

It is not enough to plant and harvest, the products must get to consumers who are willing to pay the right price for your produce.

Getting the products to the market is therefore non-negotiable, if you want to remain in business.

Having got all the stages of cultivation right, you must know your best market and off-takers.

As the owner of the farm, you are the Chief Marketing Officer of your products. You must do everything in your power to market your products. Even when your products are in high demand, you still need to market them.

In this day and age, leverage on the use of technology. Agric business is technologically driven not just in terms of operations but in marketing of your agricultural produce. Hence, use your website and social media platforms to sell your products.

> AS THE OWNER OF THE FARM, YOU'RE THE CHIEF MARKETING OFFICER OF YOUR PRODUCTS. YOU MUST DO EVERYTHING IN YOUR POWER TO MARKET YOUR PRODUCTS EVEN WHEN YOUR PRODUCTS ARE IN HIGH DEMAND.

At the startup stage, if you can't afford the services of fulltime marketers, engage the services of part time marketers. The job description of the marketers may range from marketing your produce to industries, exporters to facilitating contact with off takers and processors.

In addition, you can market your produce by registering with trade associations of the products you are cultivating. You can persuade these trade associations to visit your farm and buy your produce.

These trade associations have specific days they hold their general meetings. Consider attending their meetings and register with them as a seller.

Depending on the size of what you are producing in the farm, if it is of industrial usage, you can approach and network with companies who will be interested in your products.

Though some of these companies have strict specification which you must abide by, it will be worth your while.

Don't wait until after harvest to market. Start marketing once you start putting seeds into the ground.

If you are cultivating exportable products, contact interested exporters and intimate them of what you have on your farm.

In marketing, value-added service is crucial. Make things convenient for your customers and off-takers. This can be achieved, for example, by conveying the produce to them in your truck and net off the cost of transportation instead of waiting for them to come to your farm.

Working with Off-takers

Off-takers are very important to the business of a farmer. In relating with them however, you must exhibit high level of patience because many of them, at times, are oblivious of the level of work and sacrifice you have made before the produce became available.

I have seen farmers and buyers fighting on the farm because the buyer is offering a ridiculous price that is not commensurate with the cost of production.

To avoid this, you must market your products before they are harvested. Don't work on the assumption that people will need your produce and beat a path to your door. Your products may waste away on the farm with nobody to buy.

> DON'T WAIT UNTIL AFTER HARVEST TO MARKET. START MARKETING ONCE YOU START PUTTING SEEDS INTO THE GROUND.

This is simply because some farm produce are supposed to be harvested fresh while some have longer gestation period.

Negotiate!

I cannot overemphasize the power of negotiating skills. As a farmer, you must be a good negotiator, if not, you will discover that you will be running at a loss.

The starting point of building negotiating skills is by keeping records such that you can confidently determine how much you spent cultivating and harvesting your produce.

For instance, imagine you had a hectare of land in which cassava was planted. To negotiate confidently with off-takers and other buyers of your produce, you must know how much it cost you to produce cassava on that hectare and determine your desired profit margin.

If you spent N100, 000 to produce and a buyer is offering N100, 000 or below on that produce, then you will realize that offer was not a deal.

Every offer must be scrutinized in order to get the best deal. It is your record of expenses that will come to your rescue when you're negotiating with buyers.

From experience, everyone on the value chain wants the best of returns. That is the reason, most times, that farmers and producers gain less than the off-takers because of lack of negotiation skills.

I repeat, successful negotiation is not possible without adequate record of your expenses. This, in my opinion, is what made the farmers of old, wretched and poor!

Many farmers of old, could not adequately figure out how much it cost them to produce and at the point of sale, the buyers cheat and underprice them by preying on their ignorance, hunger for money, desperation and fear of the products perishing!

Succeeding as a farmer in this age will demand good book keeping knowledge and good negotiating skills.

You must at no point be under pressure to sell your produce. Accordingly, that is the reason you need to be a good marketer so that you can have several options and nobody is holding you to ransom. As a farmer, you need to be able to sell your products through several options.

Negotiation skills will make you maximize profits, reduce loss and expand your operations.

Securing Your Investment

After laboring to set up your farm, you need to put structures in place to secure your investment.

There are several ways of securing your investment. Among them is Community relations which we discussed in the last chapter.

Next is insurance. In this age, insuring your farm is a very good way of securing your investment.

The insurance premium rate in Nigeria is still very small - about 2% of the cost of production.

So, if your farm is costing you about N1, 000,000 to set up you are paying about N20, 000 to insure your investment. I think this is a great deal considering the risks associated with agricultural business in Nigeria.

Many insurance firms in Nigeria provide agriculture insurance services. Walk into any of their offices to get further information.

You may also consider Nigerian Agricultural Insurance Corporation (NAIC) which was established by the Federal Government of Nigeria specifically to provide agricultural risk insurance cover to Nigerian farmers.

An agro-investment as low as ₦10, 000.00 can attract a NAIC cover.

According to information available on their website, NAIC settles claims 72 hours after the execution of a Discharge Voucher and is forwarded to the claimant immediately the claim is verified.

Check http://www.naic.gov.ng for details on how to apply.

What else can you do to secure your investment? Build a farm house on the farm. The farm house will serve as a residential apartment for your members of staff.

The farm house will serve as a deterrent against theft on your farm. For instance, in a plantain plantation, most thefts are in two major categories: thieves who are hungry and looking for what to eat who will take a bunch or two; while the second set are those who will steal some bunches to sell.

If you have your farm house on the farm, the two categories of thieves would find it difficult to operate on your farm because your members of staff are within the vicinity in the farm house.

Also, on securing your investment, some people would rather want to fence round the farm. In my opinion, fencing your farm may not be a good idea.

If you have a small portion of land like one or two hectares, you can fence. But if you have an expanse of hectares like 6 upward, the money you will use to fence is enough to cultivate. It does not make commercial sense because you may want to expand in the future.

ABOUT THE AUTHOR

Banjoko Omotunde is a strategic thinker and solution minded entrepreneur, committed to always delivering the best at all times. He is a graduate of Geophysics from Olabisi Onabanjo University, Ago-Iwoye, Ogun State.

An Associate of the Institute of Strategic Management of Nigeria (ISMN), Omotunde holds an HSE 2 and HSE 3 certification in Health and Safety from the Nigeria Institute of Safety Professional (NISP). He is a trained Project Manager and an alumni of Daystar Leadership Academy, Lagos.

Omotunde has worked in several capacities in the oil and gas sector in both product distribution, interface with relevant government agencies and project execution in organizations, including;

- PM Oil marketing and sales solutions limited (2009 – 2011)
- Director at Aroma energy company limited and North Ocean Oil resources limited (2011-2014)

He now uses this wealth of experience in the marketing and distribution of quality farm produce, execution of agro-allied projects towards the expansion of the Nigerian agriculture industry.

ABOUT B.O. FARMS LTD

B.O. Farms limited is Nigeria's premier farming management, consulting, and food processing company that is aimed to be the best food production and packaging company in Africa. Banjoko Omotunde Farms Limited is registered as a limited liability company with the Nigerian Corporate Affairs Commission. The company is typically into production of different crops including but not limited to Vegetables, Plantain, Cocoa, Livestocks etc.

Farm Management Arm
This arm of our business handles setting up of farms or area of business interest in the agriculture value chain for clients. This take care of those interested in this industry who do not have the time and technical know-how to go about it.

We basically turn dreams and conceptualised ideas into reality. And set up systems to keep them running for the clients while under our management supervision for the clients for an agreed period of time to aid maximum output and profitability.

We handle this operation from the acquisition of required facility or land either on outright purchase or lease.

We oversee operations from acquisition, planting, farm monitoring, harvesting and sales of produce. Our management service is done in conjunction with several professionals and institutions to aid the best output.

CONTACT DETAILS
12, Oremeta Street, Oregun, Ikeja, Lagos.
Orunwa/Idode town, ijebu-ode, Ogun State.
Phone: +2348073312579 +2347082233044

www.ingramcontent.com/pod-product-compliance
Lightning Source LLC
Chambersburg PA
CBHW020450220526
45464CB00002B/942